Teach Yourself VISUALLY™
Word 2003

Visual™

From
maranGraphics®

&

Wiley Publishing, Inc.

Teach Yourself VISUALLY™ Word 2003

Published by
Wiley Publishing, Inc.
909 Third Avenue
New York, NY 10022

Published simultaneously in Canada

Copyright©2003 by maranGraphics, Inc.
     5755 Coopers Avenue
     Mississauga, Ontario, Canada
     L4Z 1R9

Library of Congress Control Number: 2003109655

ISBN: 0-7645-3997-3

Manufactured in the United States of America

10 9 8 7 6 5 4 3 2 1

1K/SW/RS/QT/MG

Trademark Acknowledgments

maranGraphics Inc. has attempted to include trademark information for products, services and companies referred to in this guide. Although maranGraphics Inc. has made reasonable efforts in gathering this information, it cannot guarantee its accuracy.

The maranGraphics logo is a trademark or registered trademark of maranGraphics, Inc.. Wiley, the Wiley Publishing logo, Visual, the Visual logo, Simplified, Master VISUALLY, Teach Yourself VISUALLY, Visual Blueprint, In an Instant, Read Less - Learn More and related trade dress are trademarks or registered trademarks of Wiley Publishing, Inc. in the United States and other countries and may not be used without written permission. All other trademarks are the property of their respective owners. maranGraphics, Inc. and Wiley Publishing, Inc. are not associated with any product or vendor mentioned in this book.

Important Numbers

For U.S. corporate orders, please call maranGraphics at 800-469-6616 or fax 905-890-9434.

For general information on our other products and services or to obtain technical support, please contact our Customer Care Department within the U.S. at 800-762-2974, outside the U.S. at 317-572-3993 or fax 317-572-4002.

Permissions

Wiley Publishing, Inc.   is a trademark of Wiley Publishing, Inc.

U.S. Corporate Sales	**U.S. Trade Sales**
Contact maranGraphics at (800) 469-6616 or fax (905) 890-9434.	Contact Wiley at (800) 762-2974 or fax (317) 572-4002.

Some comments from our readers...

"I have to praise you and your company on the fine products you turn out. I have twelve of the *Teach Yourself VISUALLY* and *Simplified* books in my house. They were instrumental in helping me pass a difficult computer course. Thank you for creating books that are easy to follow."

–Gordon Justin (Brielle, NJ)

"I commend your efforts and your success. I teach in an outreach program for the Dr. Eugene Clark Library in Lockhart, TX. Your *Teach Yourself VISUALLY* books are incredible and I use them in my computer classes. All my students love them!"

–Michele Schalin (Lockhart, TX)

"Thank you so much for helping people like me learn about computers. The Maran family is just what the doctor ordered. Thank you, thank you, thank you."

–Carol Moten (New Kensington, PA)

"I would like to take this time to compliment maranGraphics on creating such great books. Thank you for making it clear. Keep up the good work."

–Kirk Santoro (Burbank, CA)

"I write to extend my thanks and appreciation for your books. They are clear, easy to follow, and straight to the point. Keep up the good work!"

–Seward Kollie (Dakar, Senegal)

"What fantastic teaching books you have produced! Congratulations to you and your staff. You deserve the Nobel prize in Education in the Software category. Thanks for helping me to understand computers."

–Bruno Tonon (Melbourne, Australia)

"Over time, I have bought a number of your 'Read Less-Learn More' books. For me, they are THE way to learn anything easily."

–José A. Mazón (Cuba, NY)

"I was introduced to maranGraphics about four years ago and YOU ARE THE GREATEST THING THAT EVER HAPPENED TO INTRODUCTORY COMPUTER BOOKS!"

–Glenn Nettleton (Huntsville, AL)

"Compliments To The Chef!! Your books are extraordinary! Or, simply put, Extra-Ordinary, meaning way above the rest! THANK YOU THANK YOU THANK YOU! for creating these."

–Christine J. Manfrin (Castle Rock, CO)

"I'm a grandma who was pushed by an 11-year-old grandson to join the computer age. I found myself hopelessly confused and frustrated until I discovered the Visual series. I'm no expert by any means now, but I'm a lot further along than I would have been otherwise. Thank you!"

–Carol Louthain (Logansport, IN)

"Thank you, thank you, thank you...for making it so easy for me to break into this high-tech world. I now own four of your books. I recommend them to anyone who is a beginner like myself. Now... if you could just do one for programming VCR's, it would make my day!"

–Gay O'Donnell (Calgary, Alberta, Canada)

"You're marvelous! I am greatly in your debt."

–Patrick Baird (Lacey, WA)

maranGraphics is a family-run business
located near Toronto, Canada.

At **maranGraphics**, we believe in producing great computer books—one book at a time.

Each maranGraphics book uses the award-winning communication process that we have been developing over the last 25 years. Using this process, we organize screen shots, text and illustrations in a way that makes it easy for you to learn new concepts and tasks.

We spend hours deciding the best way to perform each task, so you don't have to! Our clear, easy-to-follow screen shots and instructions walk you through each task from beginning to end.

Our detailed illustrations go hand-in-hand with the text to help reinforce the information. Each illustration is a labor of love—some take up to a week to draw!

We want to thank you for purchasing what we feel are the best computer books money can buy. We hope you enjoy using this book as much as we enjoyed creating it!

Sincerely,

The Maran Family

Please visit us on the Web at:
www.maran.com

CREDITS

Author:
Ruth Maran

Word 2003 Update Director:
Kelleigh Johnson

Project Manager:
Judy Maran

Editing and Screen Captures:
Raquel Scott
Roderick Anatalio
Adam Giles

Layout Designer:
Richard Hung

Illustrator & Screen Artist:
Russ Marini

**Illustrator, Screen Artist &
Assistant Layout Designer:**
Steven Schaerer

Indexer:
Raquel Scott

**Wiley Vice President and
Executive Group Publisher:**
Richard Swadley

**Wiley Vice President and
Publisher:**
Barry Pruett

Wiley Editorial Support:
Jody Lefevere
Sandy Rodrigues
Lindsay Sandman

Post Production:
Robert Maran

ACKNOWLEDGMENTS

Thanks to the dedicated staff of maranGraphics, including
Roderick Anatalio, Adam Giles, Richard Hung,
Kelleigh Johnson, Wanda Lawrie, Jill Maran,
Judy Maran, Robert Maran, Ruth Maran,
Russ Marini, Steven Schaerer, Raquel Scott
and Roxanne Van Damme.

Finally, to Richard Maran who originated the easy-to-use graphic
format of this guide. Thank you for your inspiration and guidance.

TABLE OF CONTENTS

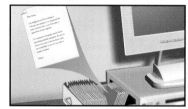

Chapter 4

Chapter 5

TABLE OF CONTENTS

Chapter 6

WORK WITH FORMATTING AND STYLES

Chapter 7

FORMAT PARAGRAPHS

Chapter 8

FORMAT PAGES

Chapter 9

PRINT DOCUMENTS

Chapter 10

WORK WITH MULTIPLE DOCUMENTS

Chapter 11

WORK WITH TABLES

TABLE OF CONTENTS

Chapter 12

WORK WITH GRAPHICS

Chapter 13

TIME-SAVING FEATURES

Chapter 14

USING MAIL MERGE

Chapter 15

USING SPEECH RECOGNITION

Chapter 16

WORD AND THE INTERNET

Word is a word processing program you can use to efficiently produce professional-looking documents, such as letters, reports, essays and newsletters.

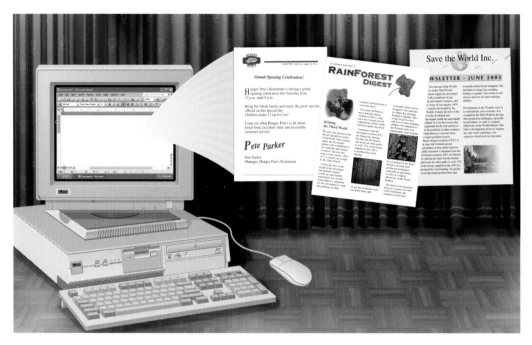

Edit Documents

Word offers many time-saving features to help you edit text in a document. You can add, delete and rearrange text. You can also quickly count the number of words in a document, check your document for spelling and grammar errors and use Word's thesaurus feature to find more suitable words.

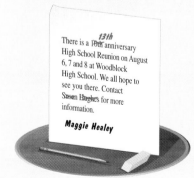

Format Documents

You can format a document to enhance the appearance of the document. You can use various fonts, styles and colors to emphasize important text. You can also adjust the spacing between lines of text, change the margins, center text on a page and create newspaper columns.

Print Documents

You can produce a paper copy of a document you create. Before printing, you can preview how the document will appear on a printed page. Word also allows you to print envelopes and labels.

Work With Tables and Graphics

Word can help you create tables to neatly display columns of information in a document. Word's ready-to-use designs allow you to instantly give a table a professional appearance. You can also add graphics, such as AutoShapes, clip art images and diagrams, to a document to illustrate ideas.

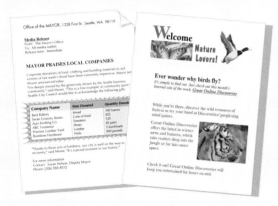

Use Mail Merge

Word's Mail Merge feature can help you quickly produce personalized letters and labels for each person on a mailing list. This is useful if you often send the same document, such as an announcement or advertisement, to many people.

Use Speech Recognition

The speech recognition feature allows you to use your voice to enter text into a document. You can also use speech recognition to select commands from menus, toolbars and dialog boxes using your voice.

Word and the Internet

Word offers features that allow you to take advantage of the Internet. You can create a hyperlink in a document to connect the document to a Web page. You can also save a document as a Web page. This allows you to place the document on the Internet for other people to view.

START WORD

When you start Word, a blank document appears on your screen. You can type text into this document.

The Getting Started task pane also appears when you start Word. You can use the task pane to quickly perform common tasks in Word.

When you finish using Word, you can exit the program. You should always exit all open programs before turning off your computer.

START WORD

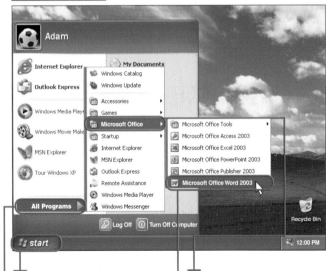

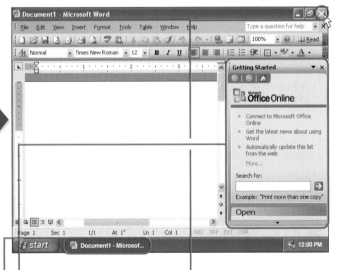

1 Click **start**.

2 Click **All Programs** to view a list of the programs on your computer.

*Note: If you are using an earlier version of Windows, click **Programs** in step 2.*

3 Click **Microsoft Office**.

4 Click **Microsoft Office Word 2003**.

■ The Microsoft Word window appears, displaying a blank document.

■ This area displays the Getting Started task pane, which allows you to quickly perform common tasks. For information on using the task pane, see page 14.

■ A button for the Microsoft Word window appears on the taskbar.

EXIT WORD

1 When you finish using Word, click ⊠ to exit Word and close the Microsoft Word window.

The Word window displays many items you can use to create and work with your documents.

Title Bar

Shows the name of the displayed document.

Menu Bar

Provides access to lists of commands available in Word and displays an area where you can type a question to get help information.

Standard Toolbar

Contains buttons you can use to select common commands, such as Save and Print.

Formatting Toolbar

Contains buttons you can use to select common formatting commands, such as Bold and Italic.

Ruler

Allows you to change tab and indent settings for your documents.

Task Pane

Contains options you can select to perform common tasks, such as opening a document.

Insertion Point

The flashing line on the screen that indicates where the text you type will appear.

Document Views

Provides access to five different views of your documents.

Scroll Bars

Allow you to browse through a document.

Status Bar

Provides information about the area of the document displayed on the screen and the position of the insertion point.

Page 1

The page displayed on the screen.

At 1"

The distance from the top of the page to the insertion point.

Sec 1

The section of the document displayed on the screen.

Ln 1

The number of lines from the top margin to the insertion point.

1/1

The page displayed on the screen and the total number of pages in the document.

Col 1

The number of characters from the left margin to the insertion point, including spaces.

ENTER TEXT

Word allows you to type text into your document quickly and easily.

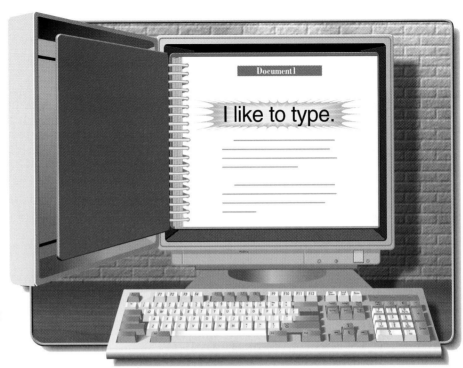

The sample documents used in each chapter of this book are available on the Web at www.maran.com/tyvword2003. You can download the sample documents so you can perform the tasks in this book without having to type the documents yourself.

ENTER TEXT

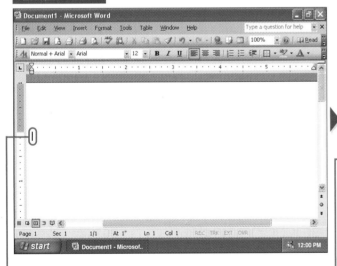

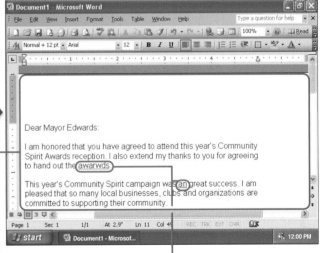

■ The text you type will appear where the insertion point flashes on your screen.

1 Type the text for your document.

Note: In this book, the font of text was changed to Arial to make the examples easier to read. To change the font of text, see page 86.

■ When you reach the end of a line, Word automatically wraps the text to the next line. You only need to press the **Enter** key when you want to start a new paragraph.

■ Word automatically underlines misspelled words in red and grammar errors in green. The underlines will not appear when you print your document. To correct misspelled words and grammar errors, see page 62.

Can I enter text anywhere in my document?

Word's Click and Type feature allows you to quickly position the insertion point in a new location so you can enter text. Double-click a blank area where you want to position the insertion point and then type the text you want to enter. The Click and Type feature is available in the Web Layout, Print Layout and Reading Layout views. To change the view, see page 36.

Why does Word automatically change the text I am typing?

Word's AutoCorrect feature automatically corrects common spelling errors as you type. For more information on the AutoCorrect feature, see page 68.

Note: To reverse a change that Word's AutoCorrect feature has made, see the top of page 69.

Error	Correction
adequit	adequate
peice	piece
recieve	receive
scedule	schedule

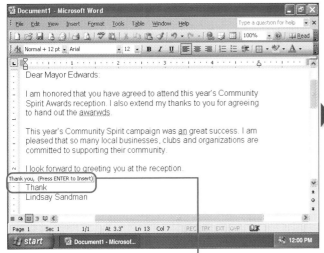

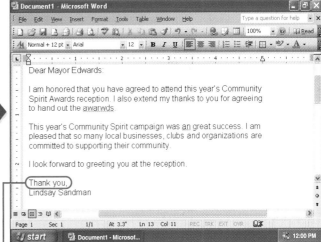

ENTER TEXT AUTOMATICALLY

■ Word's AutoText feature helps you quickly enter common words and phrases.

■ When you type the first few characters of a common word or phrase, a yellow box appears, displaying the text.

1 To insert the text, press the `Enter` key.

■ To ignore the text, continue typing.

Note: For more information on the AutoText feature, see page 70.

SELECT TEXT

Before performing
many tasks in Word,
you must select the
text you want to work
with. Selected text
appears highlighted
on your screen.

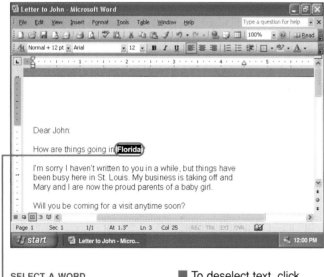

SELECT A WORD

1 Double-click the
word you want to
select. The word is
highlighted.

■ To deselect text, click
outside the selected
area.

SELECT A SENTENCE

1 Press and hold down
the `Ctrl` key as you click
the sentence you want to
select.

How do I select a paragraph or a large area of text?

To select a paragraph, position the mouse I over the paragraph you want to select and then quickly click **three** times.

To select a large area of text, click at the beginning of the text. Then press and hold down the **Shift** key as you click at the end of the text.

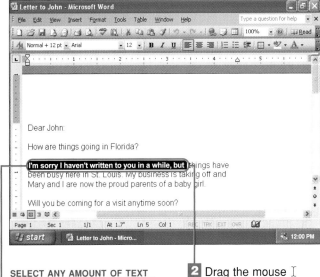

Can I select multiple areas of text in my document?

Yes. To select multiple areas of text, press and hold down the **Ctrl** key as you select each area.

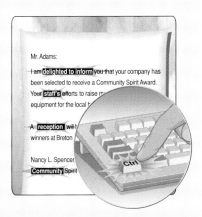

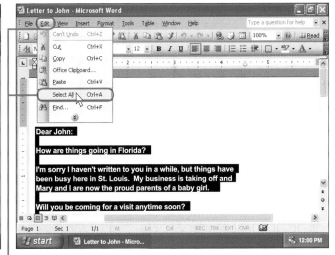

SELECT ANY AMOUNT OF TEXT

1 Position the mouse I over the first word you want to select.

2 Drag the mouse I over the text you want to select.

SELECT ENTIRE DOCUMENT

1 Click **Edit**.

2 Click **Select All** to select all the text in your document.

*Note: You can also press and hold down the **Ctrl** key as you press the **A** key to select all the text in your document.*

MOVE THROUGH A DOCUMENT

You can easily move to another location in your document.

If your document contains a lot of text, your computer screen may not be able to display all the text at once. You must scroll through your document to view other parts of the document.

MOVE THROUGH A DOCUMENT

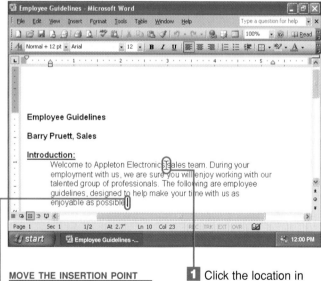

MOVE THE INSERTION POINT

■ The flashing line on your screen, called the insertion point, indicates where the text you type will appear.

1 Click the location in your document where you want to place the insertion point.

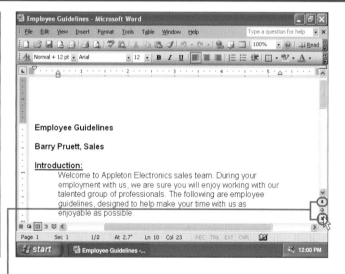

DISPLAY PREVIOUS OR NEXT PAGE

1 To display the previous or next page, click one of the following buttons.

⬆ Display previous page

⬇ Display next page

How can I use my keyboard to move through a document?

One character or line at a time

■ Press the ←, →, ↑ or ↓ key to move through a document one character or line at a time.

Note: In Reading Layout view, these keys allow you to move through the document one page at a time. For more information on the Reading Layout view, see page 44.

One screen or page at a time

■ Press the `Page Up` or `Page Down` key to move through a document one screen or page at a time.

Beginning or end of the document

■ Press and hold down the `Ctrl` key as you press the `Home` key to move to the beginning of the document.

■ Press and hold down the `Ctrl` key as you press the `End` key to move to the end of the document.

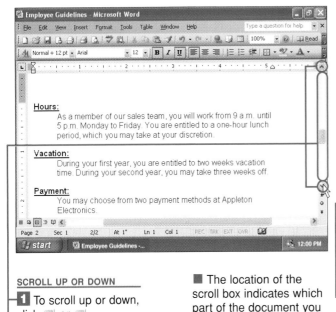

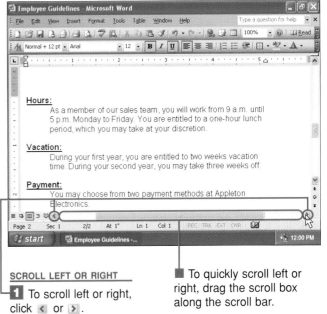

SCROLL UP OR DOWN

1 To scroll up or down, click ▲ or ▼.

■ To quickly scroll up or down, drag the scroll box along the scroll bar.

■ The location of the scroll box indicates which part of the document you are viewing. To view the middle of the document, drag the scroll box halfway down the scroll bar.

SCROLL LEFT OR RIGHT

1 To scroll left or right, click ◄ or ►.

■ To quickly scroll left or right, drag the scroll box along the scroll bar.

SELECT COMMANDS

You can select a command from a menu or toolbar to perform a task in Word. Each command performs a different task.

When you first start Word, the most commonly used commands and buttons appear on each menu and toolbar. As you work, Word customizes the menus and toolbars to display the commands and buttons you use most often.

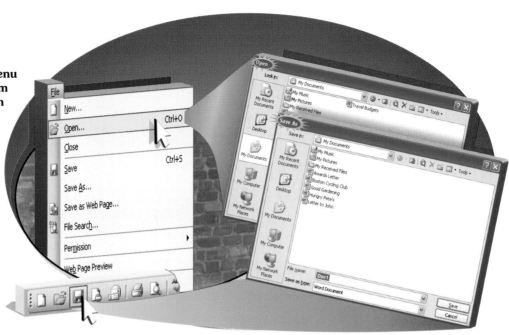

SELECT COMMANDS

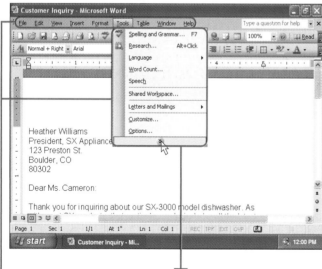

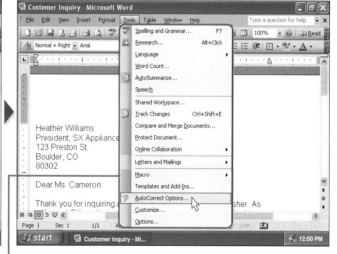

USING MENUS

1 Click the name of the menu you want to display.

■ A short version of the menu appears, displaying the most commonly used commands.

2 To expand the menu and display all the commands, position the mouse over ⚈.

■ The expanded menu appears, displaying all the commands.

3 Click the command you want to use.

Note: A dimmed command is currently not available.

■ To close a menu without selecting a command, click outside the menu.

How can I make a command appear on the short version of a menu?

When you select a command from an expanded menu, the command is automatically added to the short version of the menu. The next time you display the short version of the menu, the command you selected will appear.

Expanded Menu   **Short Menu**

How can I quickly select a command?

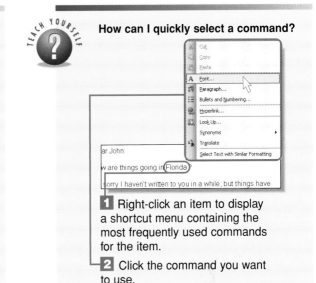

1 Right-click an item to display a shortcut menu containing the most frequently used commands for the item.

2 Click the command you want to use.

■ To close a shortcut menu without selecting a command, click outside the menu.

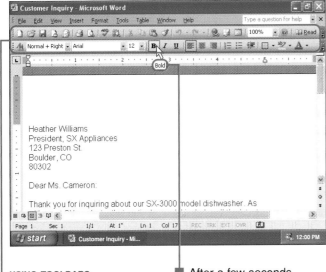

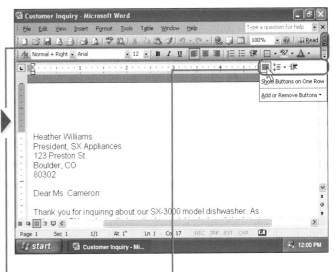

USING TOOLBARS

1 To display the name of a toolbar button, position the mouse over the button.

■ After a few seconds, the name of the button appears in a yellow box. The button name can help you determine the task the button performs.

2 A toolbar may not be able to display all its buttons. Click to display additional buttons for the toolbar.

■ Additional buttons for the toolbar appear.

3 To use a toolbar button to select a command, click the button.

USING THE TASK PANE

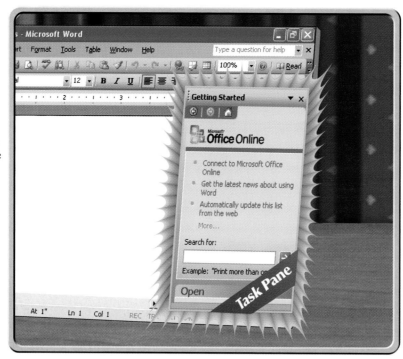

You can use the task pane to perform common tasks in Word. The Getting Started task pane appears each time you start Word.

You can display or hide the task pane at any time. When you perform some tasks, such as searching for a document, the task pane will automatically appear.

USING THE TASK PANE

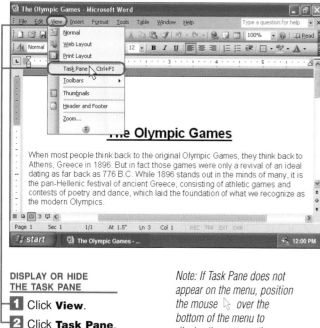

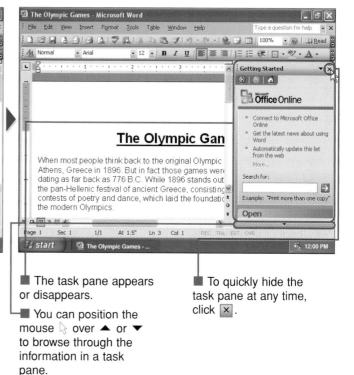

DISPLAY OR HIDE THE TASK PANE

1 Click **View**.

2 Click **Task Pane**.

Note: If Task Pane does not appear on the menu, position the mouse ⩗ over the bottom of the menu to display the menu option.

■ The task pane appears or disappears.

■ You can position the mouse ⩗ over ▲ or ▼ to browse through the information in a task pane.

■ To quickly hide the task pane at any time, click ☒.

What are some of the task panes available in Word?

Getting Started

Allows you to open documents and create new documents. For information on opening a document, see page 24.

Clipboard

Displays each item you have selected to move or copy. For information on moving and copying text, see page 52.

Clip Art

Allows you to add clip art images to your documents. For information on adding clip art images, see page 218.

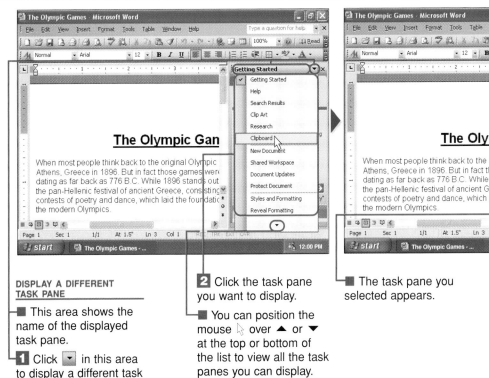

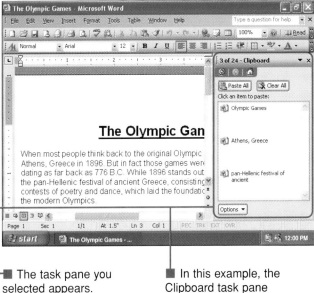

DISPLAY A DIFFERENT TASK PANE

■ This area shows the name of the displayed task pane.

1 Click ▼ in this area to display a different task pane.

2 Click the task pane you want to display.

■ You can position the mouse ⬚ over ▲ or ▼ at the top or bottom of the list to view all the task panes you can display.

■ The task pane you selected appears.

■ In this example, the Clipboard task pane appears.

GETTING HELP

If you do not know how to perform a task in Word, you can search for help information on the task.

Some help information is only available on the Internet. You must be connected to the Internet to access online help information.

GETTING HELP

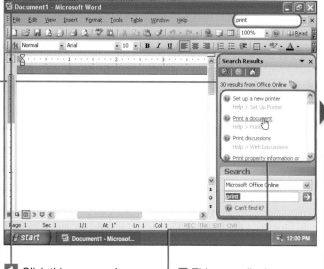

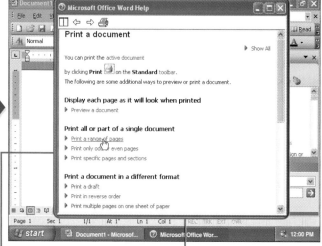

1 Click this area and type the task you want to get help information on. Then press the **Enter** key.

■ The Search Results task pane appears.

■ This area displays a list of related help topics. You can use the scroll bar to browse through the available topics.

2 Click the help topic of interest.

■ A window appears, displaying information about the help topic you selected.

3 To display additional information for a word or phrase that appears in color, click the word or phrase.

What do the icons beside each help topic represent?

Here are some icons you will see beside help topics.

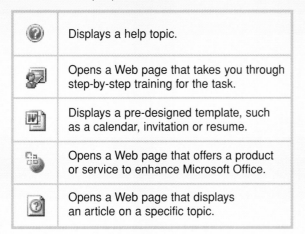	Displays a help topic.
	Opens a Web page that takes you through step-by-step training for the task.
	Displays a pre-designed template, such as a calendar, invitation or resume.
	Opens a Web page that offers a product or service to enhance Microsoft Office.
	Opens a Web page that displays an article on a specific topic.

 How can I get help information when working with a dialog box?

You can click ❓ in the top right corner of a dialog box. A window will appear, displaying help information for the dialog box.

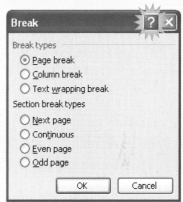

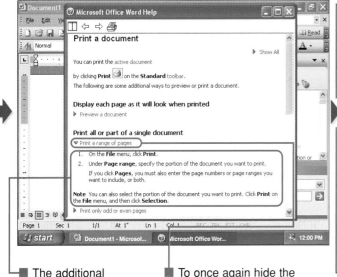

■ The additional information appears.

Note: Selecting a colored word or phrase will display information such as a definition, tip or list of steps.

■ To once again hide the information, click the colored word or phrase.

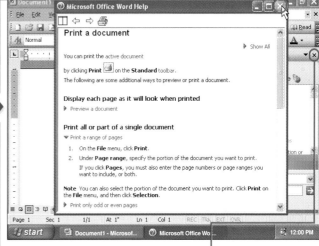

4 When you finish reviewing the help information, click ☒ to close the window.

■ To display the information for another help topic, click the help topic.

5 When you are finished getting help, click ☒ to close the Search Results task pane.

CHAPTER 2

Save and Open Documents

Are you wondering how to save, close or open a Word document? Learn how in this chapter.

SAVE A DOCUMENT

You can save your document to store it for future use. Saving a document allows you to later review and edit the document.

SAVE A DOCUMENT

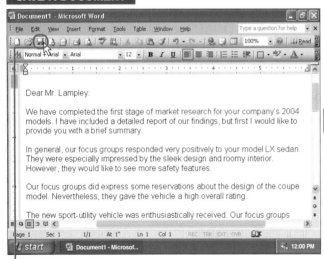

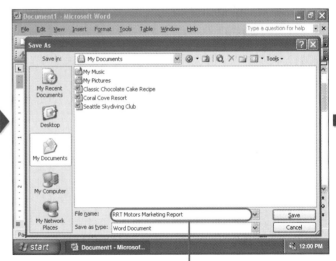

1 Click 🖫 to save your document.

Note: If 🖫 is not displayed, click 🗘 on the Standard toolbar to display the button.

■ The Save As dialog box appears.

Note: If you previously saved your document, the Save As dialog box will not appear since you have already named the document.

2 Type a name for the document.

Note: A document name cannot contain the * : ? > < | or " characters.

What are the commonly used locations that I can access?

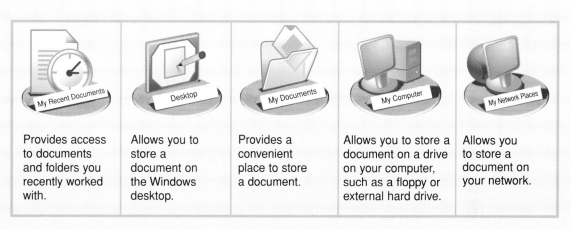

My Recent Documents

Provides access to documents and folders you recently worked with.

Desktop

Allows you to store a document on the Windows desktop.

My Documents

Provides a convenient place to store a document.

My Computer

Allows you to store a document on a drive on your computer, such as a floppy or external hard drive.

My Network Places

Allows you to store a document on your network.

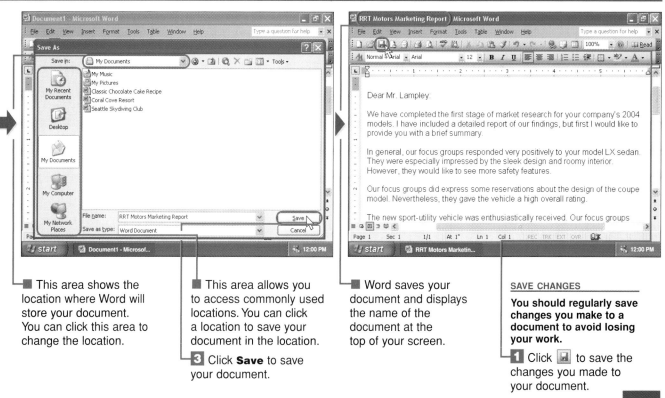

■ This area shows the location where Word will store your document. You can click this area to change the location.

■ This area allows you to access commonly used locations. You can click a location to save your document in the location.

3 Click **Save** to save your document.

■ Word saves your document and displays the name of the document at the top of your screen.

SAVE CHANGES

You should regularly save changes you make to a document to avoid losing your work.

1 Click 🖫 to save the changes you made to your document.

SAVE A DOCUMENT IN A DIFFERENT FORMAT

You can save a Word document in a different format. This is useful if you need to share a document with a colleague who does not use Word 2003.

SAVE A DOCUMENT IN A DIFFERENT FORMAT

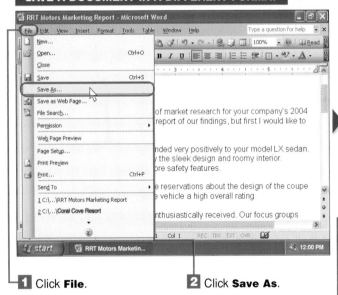

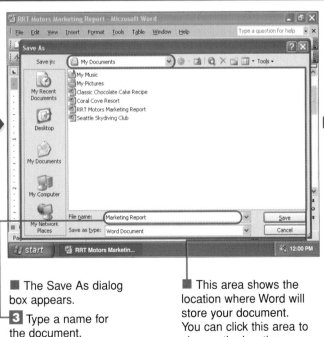

1 Click **File**.

2 Click **Save As**.

■ The Save As dialog box appears.

3 Type a name for the document.

*Note: A document name cannot contain the * : ? > < | or " characters.*

■ This area shows the location where Word will store your document. You can click this area to change the location.

**Why does a dialog box appear
when I try to save my document
in a different format?**

A dialog box appears if Word needs
to install software before saving the
document in the new format. Click
Yes to install the software.

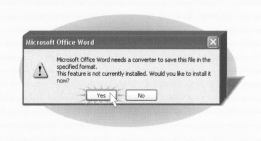

**What format should I use to save a document
that I want to share with people who use a
recent version of Microsoft Word?**

The Word 2003, 2002, 2000 and 97 programs
all use the same document format. If you want
to share your documents with people who use
Word 2002, 2000 or 97, you can save your
documents in the default **Word Document**
format.

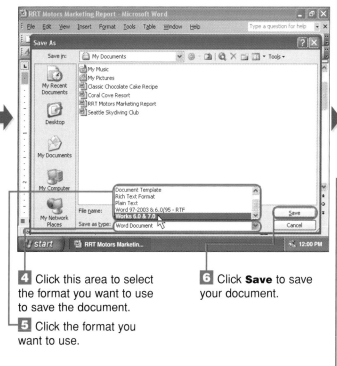

4 Click this area to select
the format you want to use
to save the document.

5 Click the format you
want to use.

6 Click **Save** to save
your document.

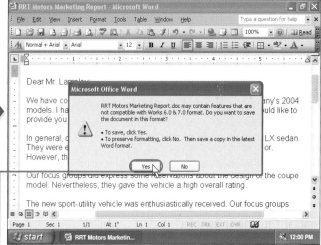

■ A dialog box may
appear, indicating that
some of the formatting
in your document may
be lost when you save
the document in the
new format.

7 Click **Yes** to continue.

*Note: If a different dialog box
appears, click **Yes** or **OK** to save
the document in the new format.*

■ Word saves your document
in the new format. You can
now open and work with the
document in another program.

OPEN A DOCUMENT

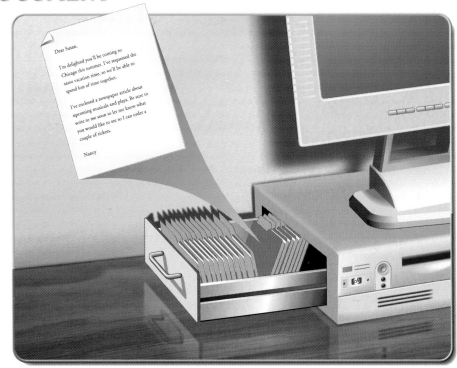

You can open a saved document to view the document on your screen. Opening a document allows you to review and make changes to the document.

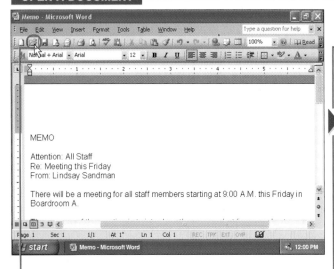

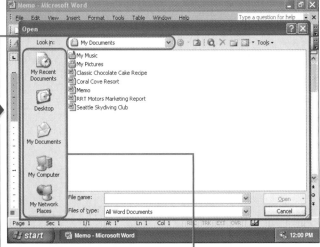

1 Click 📂 to open a document.

Note: If 📂 does not appear, click ⁝ on the Standard toolbar to display the button.

■ The Open dialog box appears.

■ This area shows the location of the displayed documents. You can click this area to change the location.

■ This area allows you to access documents in commonly used locations. You can click a location to display the documents stored in the location.

Note: For information on the commonly used locations, see the top of page 21.

How can I quickly open a document I recently worked with?

Word remembers the names of the last four documents you worked with. You can use the Getting Started task pane or the File menu to quickly open any of these documents.

Note: The Getting Started task pane appears each time you start Word. To display the Getting Started task pane, see page 14.

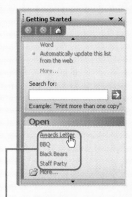

Use the Task Pane

1 Click the name of the document you want to open.

Note: If the name of the document is not displayed, position the mouse over the bottom of the task pane to display the name.

Use the File Menu

1 Click **File**.

2 Click the name of the document you want to open.

Note: If the name of the document you want is not displayed, position the mouse over the bottom of the menu to display the name.

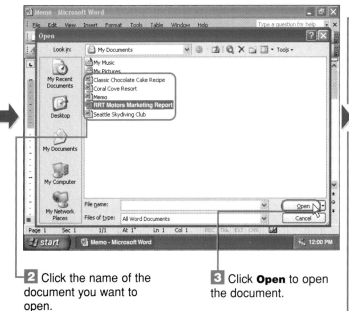

2 Click the name of the document you want to open.

3 Click **Open** to open the document.

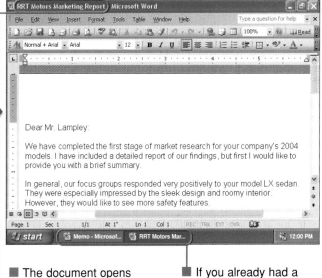

■ The document opens and appears on your screen. You can now review and make changes to the document.

■ This area displays the name of the document.

Note: To close a document, see page 187.

■ If you already had a document open, the new document appears in a new Microsoft Word window. You can click the buttons on the taskbar to switch between the open documents.

OPEN A DOCUMENT IN A DIFFERENT FORMAT

You can use Word to open and work with a document that was created in another program. This helps you work with documents from colleagues who use different word processing programs.

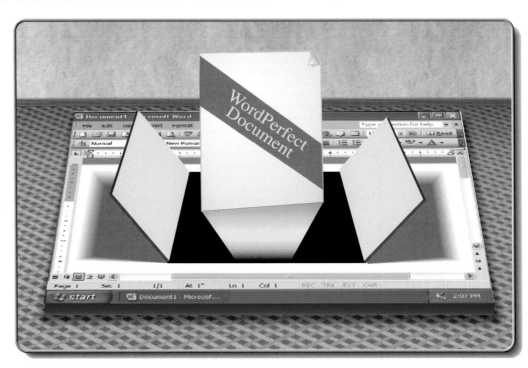

OPEN A DOCUMENT IN A DIFFERENT FORMAT

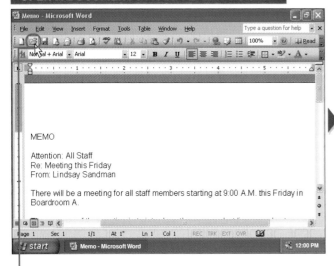

1 Click 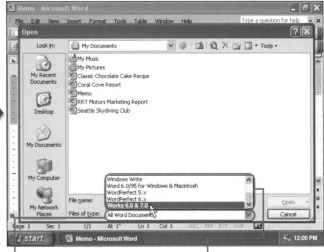 to open a document.

Note: If [icon] is not displayed, click [icon] on the Standard toolbar to display the button.

■ The Open dialog box appears.

2 Click this area to select the format of the document you want to open.

3 Click the format of the document you want to open.

*Note: If you do not know the format of the document you want to open, click **All Files**.*

26

Why does a dialog box appear when I try to open a document in a different format?

A dialog box appears if Word needs to install software before opening the document. Click **Yes** to install the software.

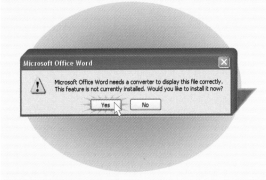

What types of documents can I open in Word?

You can open documents created in many different programs, such as WordPerfect, Windows Write, Word for Macintosh and older versions of Word for Windows.

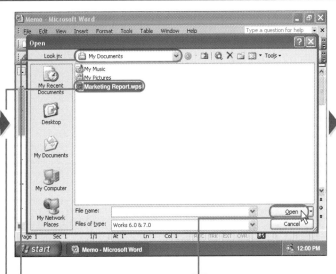

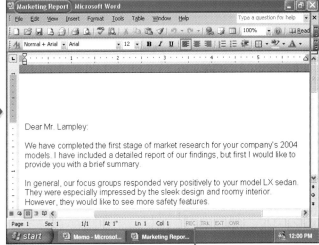

■ This area shows the location of the displayed documents. You can click this area to change the location.

4 Click the name of the document you want to open.

5 Click **Open** to open the document.

Note: If a dialog box appears on your screen, see the top of this page.

■ The document opens and appears on your screen. You can now review and make changes to the document.

■ This area displays the name of the document.

Note: To close a document, see page 187.

SEARCH FOR A DOCUMENT

If you cannot remember the name or location of a document you want to work with, you can search for the document.

SEARCH FOR A DOCUMENT

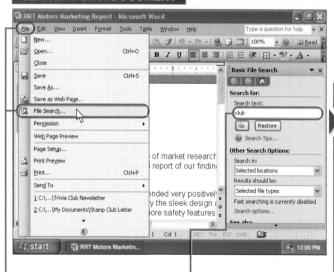

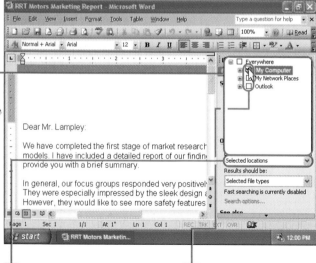

1 Click **File**.

2 Click **File Search** to search for a document.

■ The Basic File Search task pane appears.

3 Click this area and type one or more words you want to search for.

Note: If this area already contains text, drag the mouse I over the existing text and then press the Delete *key before performing step 3.*

4 Click ⌄ in this area to select the locations you want to search.

■ A check mark (✔) appears beside each location that Word will search.

Note: By default, Word will search all the drives and folders on your computer.

5 You can click the box beside a location to add (☑) or remove (☐) a check mark.

6 Click outside the list of locations to close the list.

How will Word use the words I specify to search for documents?

Word will search the contents of documents and the file names of documents for the words you specify. When searching the contents of documents, Word will search for various forms of the words. For example, searching for "run" will find "run," "running" and "ran."

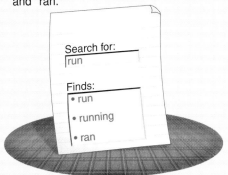

When selecting the locations and types of files I want to search for, how can I display more items?

Each item that displays a plus sign (⊞) contains hidden items. To display the hidden items, click the plus sign (⊞) beside the item (⊞ changes to ⊟). To once again hide the items, click the minus sign (⊟) beside the item.

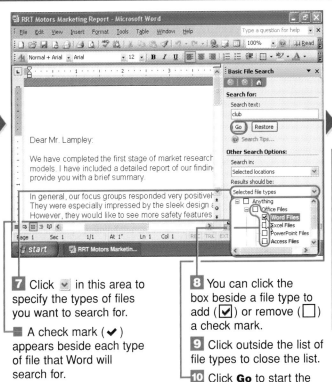

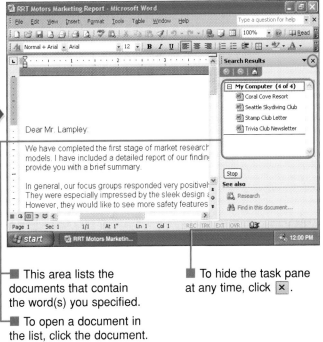

7 Click ⌄ in this area to specify the types of files you want to search for.

■ A check mark (✔) appears beside each type of file that Word will search for.

8 You can click the box beside a file type to add (✔) or remove (☐) a check mark.

9 Click outside the list of file types to close the list.

10 Click **Go** to start the search.

■ This area lists the documents that contain the word(s) you specified.

■ To open a document in the list, click the document.

■ To hide the task pane at any time, click ✕.

PROTECT A DOCUMENT

You can prevent other people from opening or making changes to a document by protecting it with a password.

PROTECT A DOCUMENT

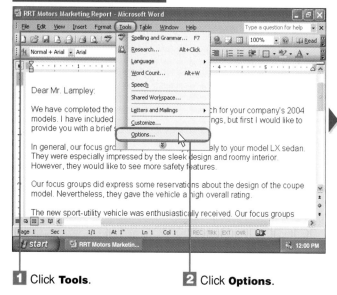

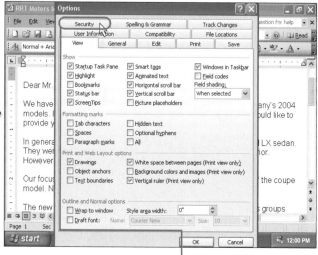

1 Click **Tools**.

2 Click **Options**.

■ The Options dialog box appears.

3 Click the **Security** tab.

What password should I use to protect my document?

When choosing a password, you should not use words that people can easily associate with you, such as your name or favorite sport. Effective passwords connect two words or numbers with a special character (example: **car#123**). A password can contain up to 15 characters and be any combination of letters, numbers and symbols.

Should I take any special precautions with my password?

You should write down your password and keep it in a safe place. If you forget the password, you may not be able to open the document.

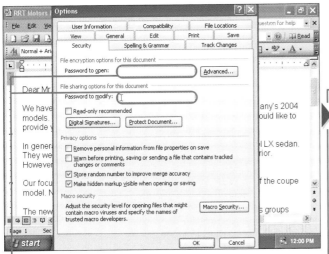

4 Click the box for the type of password you want to enter.

Password to open
Prevents people from opening the document without entering the correct password.

Password to modify
Prevents people from making changes to the document without entering the correct password.

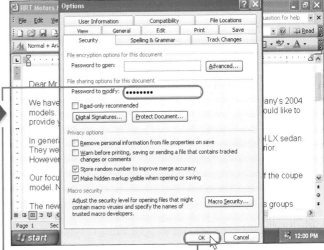

5 Type the password you want to use.

6 Click **OK** to continue.

CONTINUED

PROTECT A DOCUMENT

After you protect a document with a password, Word will ask you to enter the password each time you open the document.

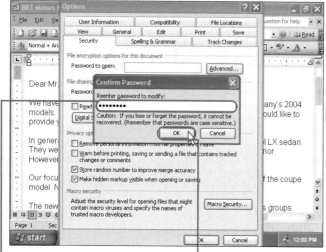

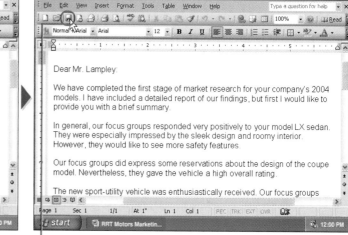

■ The Confirm Password dialog box appears, asking you to confirm the password you entered.

7 Type the password again to confirm the password.

8 Click **OK** to protect the document.

9 Click 🔲 to save the changes you made to the document.

Note: If you have not previously saved the document, the Save As dialog box will appear. To save a document, see page 20.

■ To close a document, see page 187.

I typed the correct password, but Word will not open my document. What is wrong?

Passwords in Word are case sensitive. If you do not enter the correct uppercase and lowercase letters, Word will not accept the password. For example, if your password is **car#123**, you cannot enter **Car#123** or **CAR#123** to open the document.

 How do I unprotect a document?

To unprotect a document, perform steps **1** to **6** starting on page 30, except in step **5**, drag the mouse I over the existing password until you highlight the password and then press the Delete key. Then perform step **9** below.

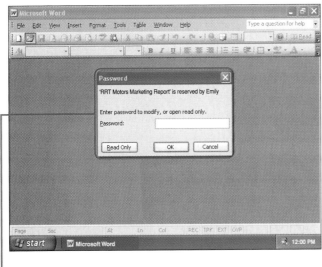

OPEN A PROTECTED DOCUMENT

■ A Password dialog box appears each time you open a protected document. To open a document, see page 24.

Note: The appearance of the dialog box depends on the type of password assigned to the document.

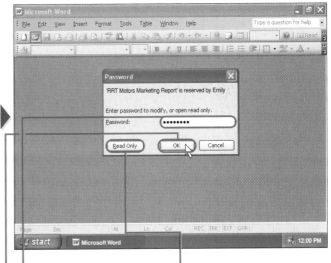

1 Type the correct password.

2 Click **OK**.

■ If the Read Only button is available, you can click the button to open the document without entering a password. You will not be able to save changes you make to the document.

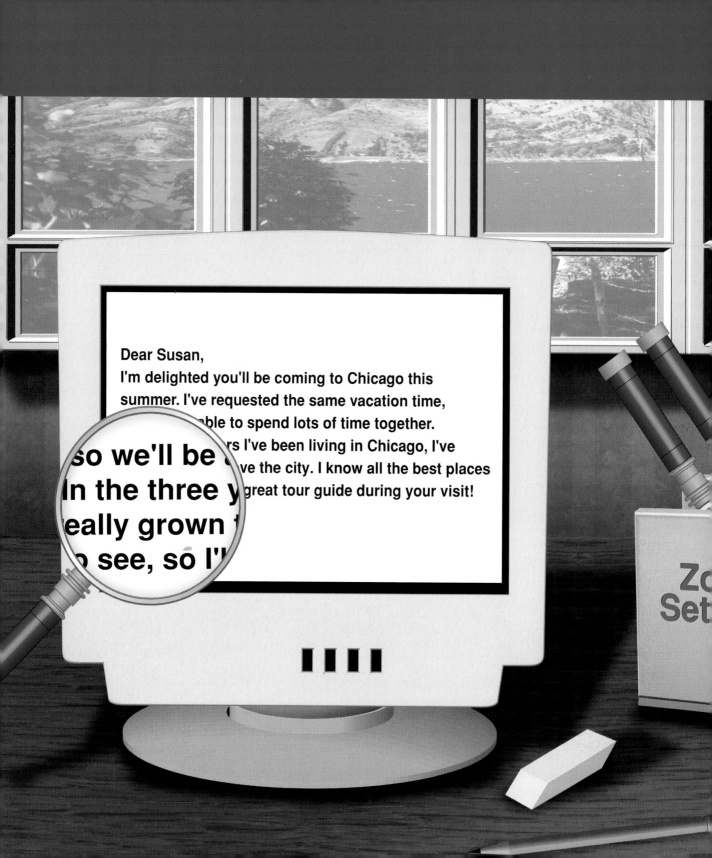

Dear Susan,
I'm delighted you'll be coming to Chicago this summer. I've requested the same vacation time, [...]ble to spend lots of time together. [...]rs I've been living in Chicago, I've [...]ve the city. I know all the best places [...]great tour guide during your visit!

so we'll be [...]
In the three y[...]
eally grown [...]
o see, so I'[...]

CHAPTER 3

Change Display of Documents

Are you interested in changing the way your document appears on your screen? In this chapter, you will learn how to display your document in a different view, display or hide a toolbar and more.

CHANGE THE VIEW OF A DOCUMENT

Word offers five different views that you can use to display your document. You can choose the view that best suits your needs.

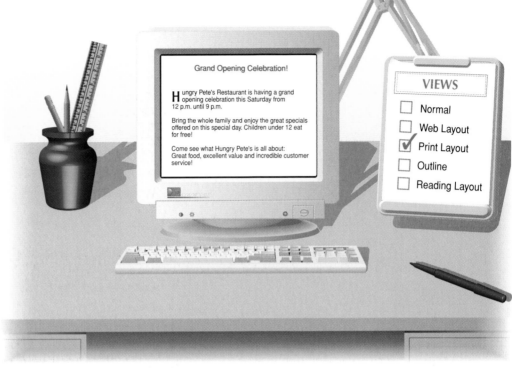

VIEWS

- ☐ Normal
- ☐ Web Layout
- ☑ Print Layout
- ☐ Outline
- ☐ Reading Layout

CHANGE THE VIEW OF A DOCUMENT

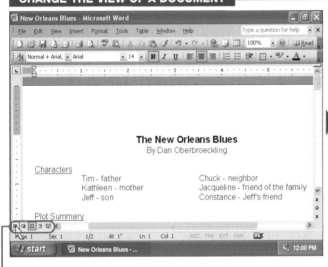

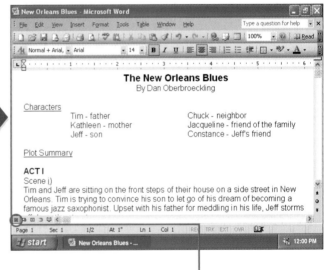

1 To change the view of your document, click one of the following buttons.

- ≣ Normal
- ▣ Web Layout
- ▣ Print Layout
- ▣ Outline
- ▥ Reading Layout

■ Your document appears in the view you selected.

■ The button for the view you selected appears orange.

Normal View

The Normal view simplifies the layout of your document so you can quickly enter, edit and format text. This view does not display certain elements in your document, such as margins and page numbers.

Web Layout View

Working in the Web Layout view is useful when you are creating a Web page or a document that you plan to view only on a computer screen.

Print Layout View

You can work in the Print Layout view when you want to see how your document will appear on a printed page. This view displays all the elements in your document, such as margins and page numbers.

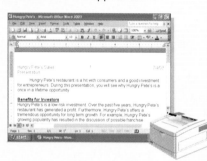

Outline View

The Outline view is useful when you want to review and work with the structure of a long document. This view allows you to collapse a document to see only the headings or expand a document to see all the headings and text.

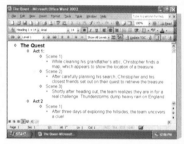

Reading Layout View

The Reading Layout view is useful when you are reading a document on screen. This view removes distracting elements and makes adjustments to the document to make it easy to read on the screen. For more information on the Reading Layout view, see page 44.

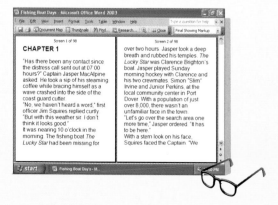

DISPLAY OR HIDE THE RULER

You can display or hide the ruler at any time. The ruler helps you position text in a document.

When you first start Word, the ruler appears on your screen.

You cannot display or hide the ruler in the Outline or Reading Layout view. For information on the views, see page 36.

DISPLAY OR HIDE THE RULER

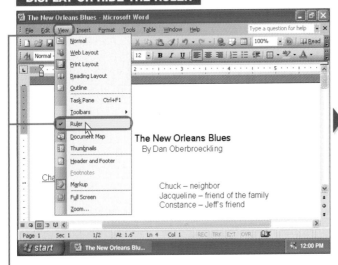

1 Click **View**.

2 Click **Ruler**. A check mark (✔) beside **Ruler** indicates the ruler is currently displayed.

Note: If Ruler does not appear on the menu, position the mouse ☐ over the bottom of the menu to display the menu option.

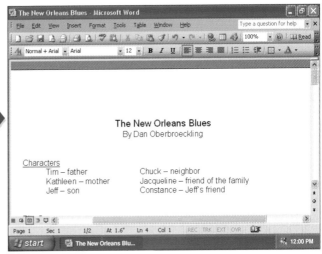

■ Word displays or hides the ruler.

Note: Hiding the ruler helps provide a larger and less cluttered working area.

DISPLAY OR HIDE A TOOLBAR

Word offers several
toolbars that you
can display or hide
to suit your needs.
Toolbars contain
buttons that you
can select to quickly
perform common
tasks.

When you first
start Word,
the **Standard**
and **Formatting**
toolbars appear
on your screen.

DISPLAY OR HIDE A TOOLBAR

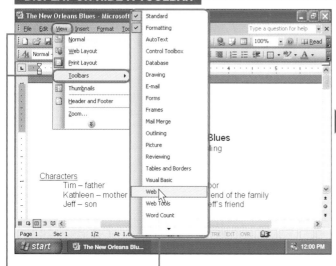

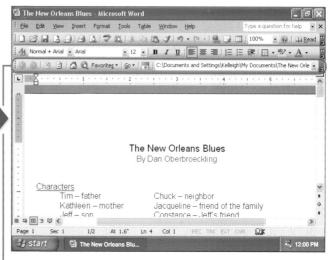

1 Click **View**.

2 Click **Toolbars**.

■ A list of toolbars appears.
A check mark (✔) appears
beside the name of each
toolbar that is currently
displayed.

3 Click the name of the
toolbar you want to display
or hide.

■ Word displays or hides
the toolbar you selected.

*Note: A screen displaying fewer
toolbars provides a larger and
less cluttered working area.*

MOVE A TOOLBAR

You can move a toolbar to the top, bottom, right or left edge of your screen.

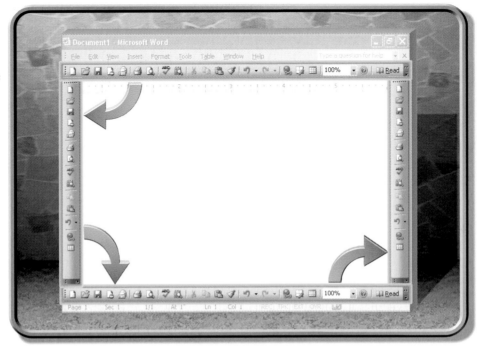

You can move a toolbar to the same row as another toolbar or to its own row.

MOVE A TOOLBAR

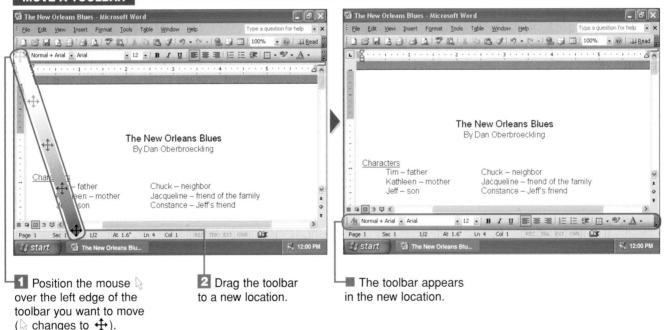

1 Position the mouse ℕ over the left edge of the toolbar you want to move (ℕ changes to ✛).

2 Drag the toolbar to a new location.

■ The toolbar appears in the new location.

RESIZE A TOOLBAR

You can increase the size of a toolbar to display more buttons on the toolbar. This is useful when a toolbar appears on the same row as another toolbar and cannot display all of its buttons.

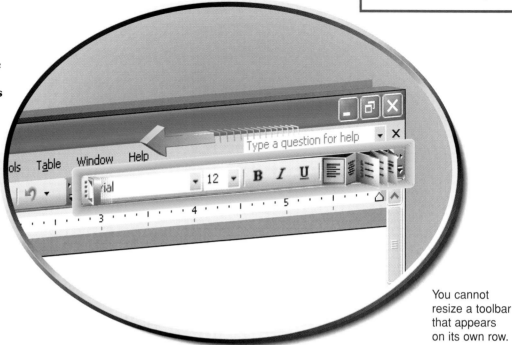

You cannot resize a toolbar that appears on its own row.

RESIZE A TOOLBAR

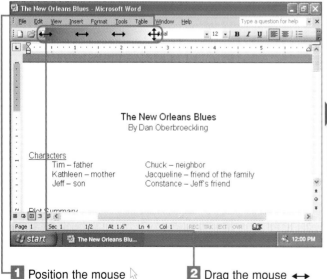

1 Position the mouse ⇖ over the left edge of the toolbar you want to resize (⇖ changes to ✥).

2 Drag the mouse ↔ until the toolbar is the size you want.

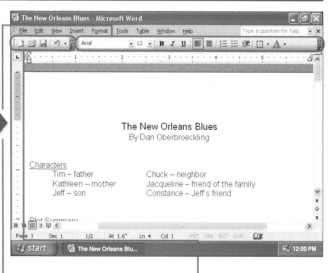

■ The toolbar displays the new size.

■ The new toolbar size affects the location and size of other toolbars on the same row.

ZOOM IN OR OUT

Word allows you to enlarge or reduce the display of text on your screen.

You can increase the zoom setting to view an area of your document in more detail or decrease the zoom setting to view more of your document at once.

The available zoom settings depend on the current view of your document. For information on the document views, see page 36.

ZOOM IN OR OUT

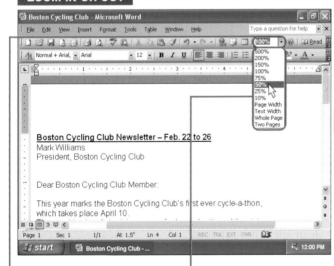

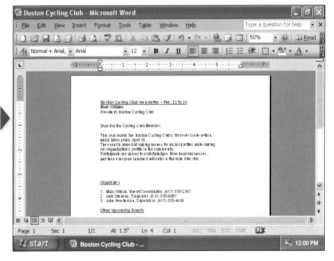

1 Click ⬝ in this area to display a list of zoom settings.

Note: If the Zoom area is not displayed, click ⬝ on the Standard toolbar to display the area.

2 Click the zoom setting you want to use.

*Note: Select **Page Width** or **Text Width** to fit the page or the text across the width of your screen. Select **Whole Page** or **Two Pages** to display one or two full pages across your screen.*

■ The document appears in the new zoom setting. You can edit the document as usual.

■ Changing the zoom setting will not affect the way text appears on a printed page.

■ To return to the normal zoom setting, repeat steps **1** and **2**, selecting **100%** in step **2**.

SPLIT A DOCUMENT

You can split your
document into
separate sections.
This allows you to
display different
areas of a long
document at the
same time.

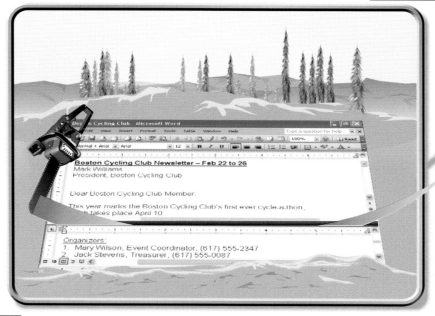

Each section of
a split document
contains a copy
of the entire
document.

SPLIT A DOCUMENT

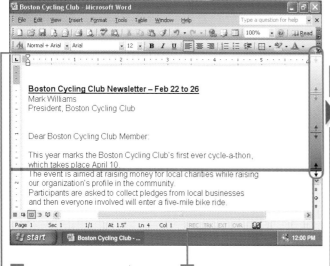

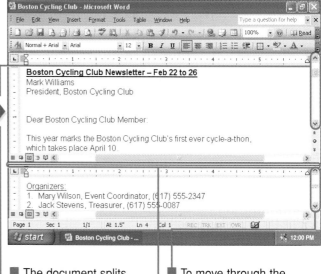

1 Position the mouse ↘
over this area (↘ changes
to ↕).

2 Drag the mouse ↕
to where you want to split
the document.

■ The document splits
into two sections.

■ To move through the
text above the dividing
line, you can use this
scroll bar.

■ To move through the
text below the dividing line,
you can use this scroll bar.

■ If you no longer want to
split the document, position
the mouse ↘ over the dividing
line (↘ changes to ↕). Then
double-click the dividing line to
remove the line from your
screen.

READ A DOCUMENT ON SCREEN

You can use the **Reading Layout** view to make a document easier to read on your screen. However, your document will no longer accurately represent how it will appear when printed.

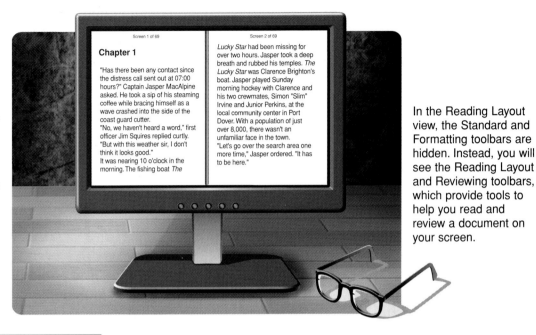

In the Reading Layout view, the Standard and Formatting toolbars are hidden. Instead, you will see the Reading Layout and Reviewing toolbars, which provide tools to help you read and review a document on your screen.

READ A DOCUMENT ON SCREEN

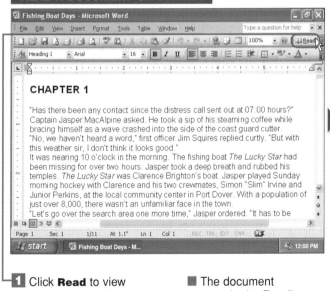

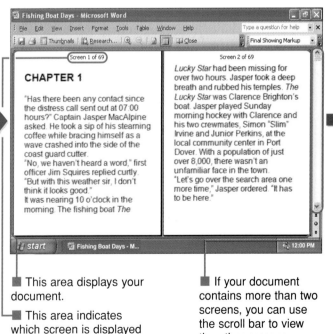

1 Click **Read** to view your document in the Reading Layout view.

Note: If the Read button is not displayed, click ⬚ on the Standard toolbar to display the button.

■ The document appears in the Reading Layout view.

■ This area displays your document.

■ This area indicates which screen is displayed and the total number of screens in your document.

■ If your document contains more than two screens, you can use the scroll bar to view the other screens.

Will Word ever automatically switch to the Reading Layout view?

When someone sends you a Word document as an attachment to an e-mail message and you open the attachment in Microsoft Outlook, Word will automatically display the document in the Reading Layout view.

Is the Reading Layout view suitable for all my documents?

The Reading Layout view may not be suitable for all your documents. For example, tables, columns or WordArt may not appear correctly. If you need to view these types of items, you should view your document in the Print Layout view instead. For more information on the Print Layout view, see page 37.

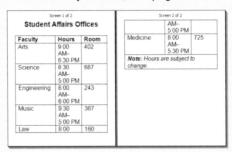

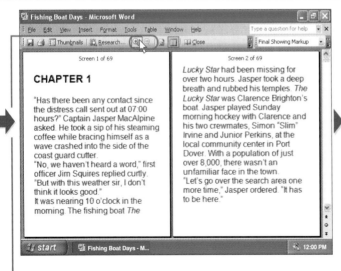

2 To change the size of the text on your screen, click one of the following buttons.

🔍 Increase the size of text

🔍 Decrease the size of text

Note: If 🔍 or 🔍 is not displayed, click ⁞ on the Reading Layout toolbar to display the buttons.

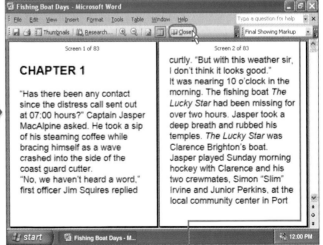

■ You can edit the document in the Reading Layout view as you would in any other view.

Note: For information on the other document views, see page 37.

3 When you finish reading your document, click **Close** to return to the previous view.

Note: If the Close button is not displayed, click ⁞ on the Reading Layout toolbar to display the button.

You can use the
Document Map
to move through
a long document.
The Document Map
displays an outline
of the document
on your screen.

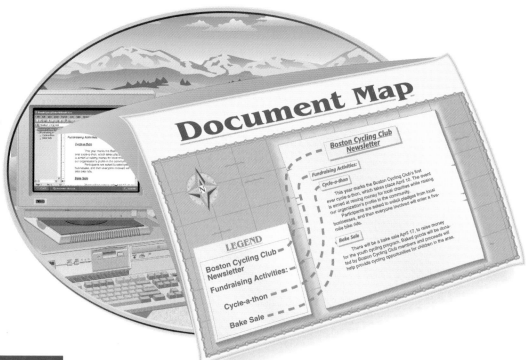

USING THE DOCUMENT MAP

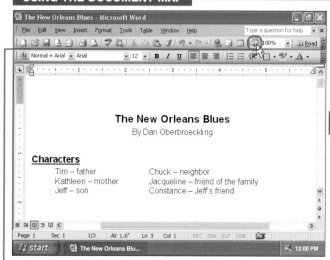

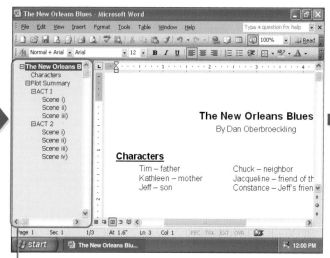

1 Click 🔍 to display
the Document Map.

*Note: If 🔍 is not displayed,
click ⁝ on the Standard
toolbar to display the button.*

■ The Document Map
appears, showing the
headings in your document.

*Note: If the Document Map does
not display headings, see the
top of page 47.*

Why doesn't the Document Map display any headings?

The Document Map appears blank if Word does not recognize any headings in your document. If you want to be able to use the Document Map to move through a document, you may need to format the headings in your document using one of the Heading styles included with Word. To apply a style included with Word, perform steps **1** to **3** starting on page 106, selecting a Heading style in step **3**.

Part of a heading in the Document Map is hidden from view. How can I display the entire heading?

To display the entire heading, position the mouse over the heading. After a few seconds, the entire heading appears in a yellow box.

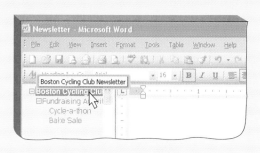

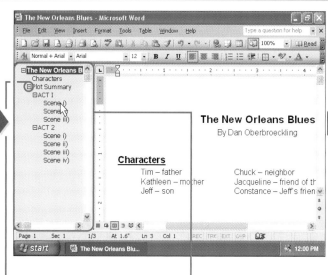

■ A minus sign (⊟) beside a heading indicates the heading has subheadings. To hide the subheadings, click the minus sign (⊟ changes to ⊞).

Note: To once again display the subheadings, click the plus sign (⊞).

2 Click a heading or subheading to instantly jump to a specific part of your document.

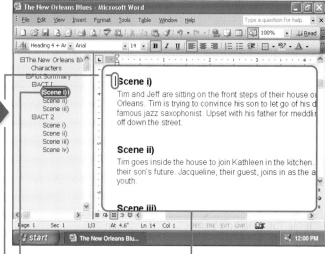

■ Word highlights the heading or subheading you selected.

■ The insertion point moves to the heading or subheading in your document.

■ This area displays the part of the document you selected.

■ To hide the Document Map, repeat step **1**.

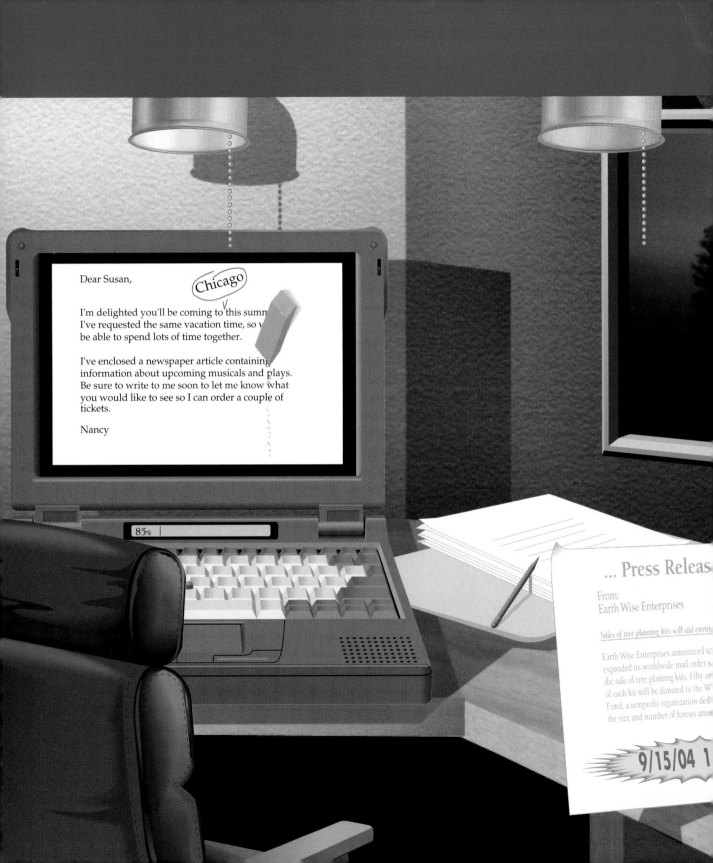